THE BEST MATCH

A Mayan Folk Tale

Retold by
Jorge Argueta

Illustrated by
Peter Martinez Grosshauser

HAMPTON-BROWN

Characters

Mama and Papa Mouse

Daughter Mouse

Mama and Papa Mouse
want to help their
daughter find a good
husband.

THE BEST MATCH

On a mountain far away, there was a family of mice. Papa and Mama Mouse loved their daughter more than anything in the world.

"She is very beautiful. She is more beautiful than the stars!" Papa Mouse said.

♪ Our Daughter
Song

Our daughter is sweet, gentle,
and bright.
She is such a beautiful sight!
She is sweeter than honey
from bees.
She is gentler than a breeze
through the trees.
She is brighter than the rays
from the Sun.
She's the sweetest, gentlest,
brightest one.

"Our daughter is special. She needs a husband to love her," Mama Mouse said.

"He must be powerful, too," Papa Mouse added.

"And kind and gentle," Daughter Mouse said.

Just then, the Moon filled the sky with light.
"Uj, the Moon, is the wisest one we know,"
said Mama Mouse. "She can help us."

"Dear Uj," Papa Mouse called to the Moon,
"our daughter needs the best husband in
the world."

"He must be kind and gentle," Daughter
Mouse added.

The Moon smiled down at the mice.

"Kin, the Sun, brings the light we need every day," the Moon said. "He is important and powerful."

"The Sun looks kind and gentle, too,"
Daughter Mouse added.

Kin, the Sun

The Sun is more important
than the flowers that grow.

The Sun is the most important
one I know.

The Sun is more powerful
than the rain that pounds.

The Sun is the most powerful
one around.

Just then, light filled the morning sky.
It was Kin, the Sun.

"Great Kin," said Papa Mouse. "You are
the most powerful one in the universe.
Will you marry our beautiful daughter?"

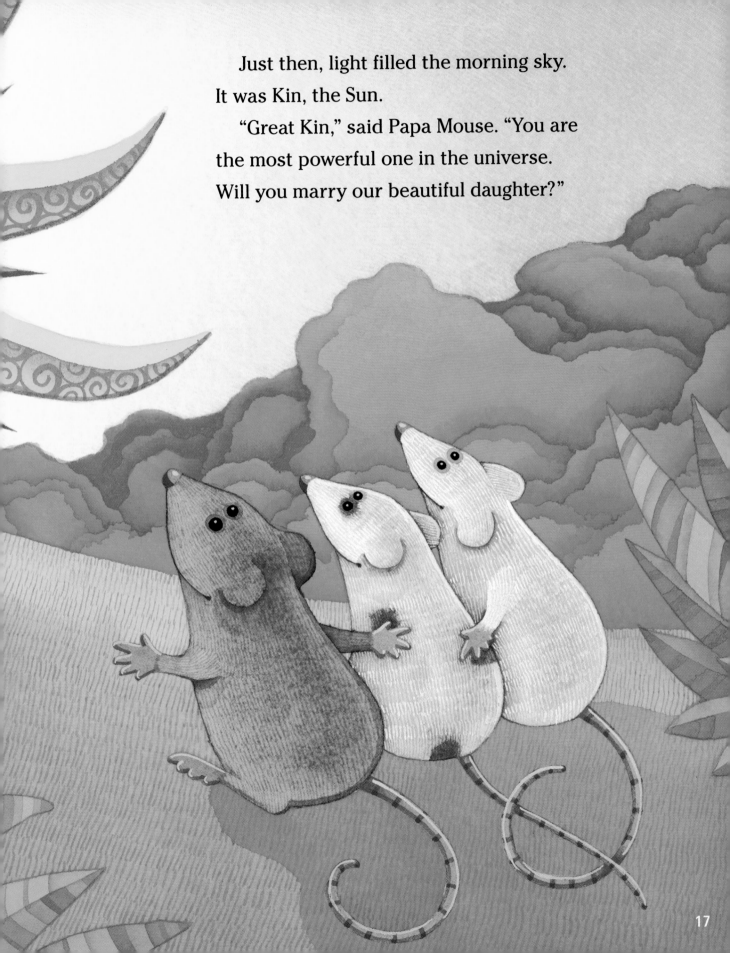

The Sun smiled. "Your daughter is more beautiful than a rainbow," he agreed. "But Tiokal, the Cloud, can block my light. He is more powerful than I am."

"The Cloud looks kind and gentle, too,"
Daughter Mouse thought.

The Wind blew through the trees.

"Greetings, Ik," Papa Mouse called. "You are greater than the Cloud and the Sun. Please marry our lovely, bright daughter."

"Your daughter is brighter than the fireflies at night," the Wind said. "But even the strongest wind cannot shake Pak, the Wall. He is stronger than I am."

"The Wall looks very kind and gentle," Daughter Mouse thought.

The Stone Wall stood in the field.

"Greetings, Pak!" Mama Mouse called.
"You are stronger than the Wind, the
Cloud, and the Sun. Please marry our
gentle daughter."

The Wall smiled. "Your daughter is
gentler than a feather," he agreed. "But
the Field Mouse can make holes in my
wall. He is more powerful than I am."

"The Field Mouse is more powerful than the Wall, the Wind, the Cloud, and the Sun. He is the greatest one of all!" Papa and Mama Mouse said.

"He is the best match for me!"
Daughter Mouse said.

Field Mouse

Field Mouse is a good match.
He is the best match of all.

He is better than the Sun.
He is better than the Wall.

He is better than the Wind
or the Cloud.

Yes, he is the best match of all!

Field Mouse is a good match.
He is the best match of all.

The Field Mouse and Daughter Mouse met. Their little hearts jumped, and their eyes melted. It was love!

Soon, the two mice were married.
What a party! It lasted for four days
and four nights.

And their love lasted forever!